Sarah ...
Jenny Doan, David ...

MANAGING EDITOR
Natalie Earnheart

CREATIVE DIRECTOR
Christine Ricks

PHOTOGRAPHER
BPD Studios

CONTRIBUTING PHOTOGRAPHERS
Jake Doan, Katie Whitt

VIDEOGRAPHER
Jake Doan

TECHNICAL WRITER
Edie McGinnis

TECHNICAL EDITOR
Jane Miller

PATTERN LAYOUT
Ally Simmons

PROJECT DESIGN TEAM
Natalie Earnheart, Jenny Doan,
Sarah Galbraith

AUTHOR OF PATCHWORK MURDER
Steve Westover

CONTRIBUTING COPY WRITERS
Jenny Doan, Natalie Earnheart, Christine
Ricks, Katie Mifsud, Cammille Maddox

COPY EDITOR
Geoff Openshaw

CONTRIBUTING PIECERS
Jenny Doan, Natalie Earnheart,
Kelly McKenzie, Carol Henderson,
Cindy Morris

CONTRIBUTING QUILTERS
Jamey Stone-Manager, Debbie Allen-
Daytime Asst. Manager, Tia Gilliam-
Nighttime Asst. Manager, Sarah Richardson,
Karen Russell, Mari Zullig, Debbie Allen,
Linda Frump, Sherry Melton, Debbie Elder,
Betty Bates, Deloris Burnett, Bernice Kelly,
Dixie Flamm, Linda Schwaninger, Daniela
Kirk, Sandi Gaunce, Kara Snow, Kayla
Youtsey, Raven Rhoads, James Evenson,
Amy Gertz, Abby Anderson

PRINTING SERVICES
Cenveo Publisher Services
2901 Byrdhill Road
Richmond, VA 23228

CONTACT US
Missouri Star Quilt Company
114 N Davis
Hamilton, Mo. 64644
888-571-1122
info@missouriquiltco.com

content

2

Ooops! Sometimes we make mistakes.
To find corrections to every issue of Block
go to: **www.msqc.co/corrections**

photo by Heidi Stock

Happy Holidays
from MSQC

"You give but little when you give of your possessions. It is when you give of yourself that you truly give." -Kahlil Gibran

My mother loves poetry, so growing up I was surrounded by it. One of Mom's favorite authors (and now mine) is Kahlil Gibran. He had a way of capturing a powerful idea in just a few words, like a snapshot of truth.

To me the Gibran quote above is so expressive of what we give when quilting. Recently my son Alan (our MSQC computer wizard) had an idea that everyone in our company ought to make a quilt. So to be an example, he set out to make the first quilt of his life. Alan has watched me quilt for years, so he thought quilting would be really easy for him. Then he opened up a layer cake and began . . .

Nothing was easy! The cutting, designing, and sewing all took plenty of work and lots of help from others. When Alan finally got the top finished he asked, "How do you quilters do this? I have never put this much time or energy into anything I have given away."

Then something changed as he put his quilt on the quilting machine and started the finishing process. As this quilt became real to him, he became giddy with excitement. He was so amazed and pleased that he had made this incredible thing!

And so quilting changes us. We start out quilting for ourselves and within a short time we are quilting to give to others. So this season I want to say thank you to you quilters for all you do. Because as we give these quilts, we give of ourselves and we change the world a little. It becomes a softer, kinder, sweeter place to be. Thank you for changing the world a stitch at a time. We love our customers!

Happy Holidays,

Jenny

JENNY DOAN
MISSOURI STAR QUILT CO

cool *yuletides*

Grab the holly berries and some mistletoe and deck the yule! The holidays are upon us and it's time to gather together as friends and family. The combination of christmasy reds, garland greens and snowy, twinkle-light white sets the mood. I'm ready to light a fire in the fireplace and put some wassail on the stove to warm. Let the festivities begin!

This year I've been feeling a cooler vibe to the holiday season. I can't wait for the snow to fall so I can throw a log on the fire. This color palette warms me right up with peppermint reds and blue-green greenery. I hope it does the same for you. We here at MSQC all wish you the very merriest of holidays. Make something beautiful.

CHRISTINE RICKS
MSQC Creative Director, BLOCK MAGAZINE

SOLIDS

FBY28328   Modern Background Paper - Handwriting Silver on White by Zen Chic for Moda Fabrics
SKU: 1580 12

FBY14555   Designer Solids - Pearl
by Free Spirit Fabrics for Free Spirit Fabrics SKU: CSFSESS.PEARL

FBY14534   Designer Solids - Light Jade
by Free Spirit Fabrics for Free Spirit Fabrics
SKU: CSFSESS.LTJDE

FBY12988   Cotton Supreme Solids - Turks and Calicos
by RJR Fabrics for RJR Fabrics
SKU: 9617-292

FBY12939   Cotton Supreme Solids - Hot Pink
by RJR Fabrics for RJR Fabrics
SKU: 9617-217

FBY8537   Cotton Supreme Solids - Redwork
by RJR Fabrics for RJR Fabrics
SKU: 9617-222

PRINTS

FBY32016   Dot.Dot.Dash-! - Dot Stripe Pink
by Me & My Sister for Moda Fabrics
SKU: 22265 11

FBY32024   Dot.Dot.Dash-! - Dot Stripe Turquoise
by Me & My Sister for Moda Fabrics
SKU: 22265 16

FBY30597   Lucky Strikes - Scorecard Blue Green
by Kimberly Kight for Cotton+Steel
SKU: 3020-3

FBY32162   Simply Colorful II - Blue Modern Geometric XOXO Teal by V & Co. for Moda Fabrics
SKU: 10855 17

FBY32015   Dot.Dot.Dash-! - Stripe in a Stripe Pink
by Me & My Sister for Moda Fabrics
SKU: 22266 11

FBY32190   Winter Essentials III - Winter Village Red
by Studio E for Studio E
SKU: 2968-88

jack & jill

quilt designed by JENNY DOAN

One year, my boys decided to make some Christmas money by selling mistletoe. Luckily, we had a friend who owned a ranch, and many of the trees on his property had mistletoe growing on them. As mistletoe is effectively a parasite and can kill the tree to which it is attached, our friend was all too happy to donate the mistletoe to the boys. So with visions of sugarplums and extra spending money dancing in their heads, off they went. They started out so excited about their brilliant idea, but it didn't take long to realize that this project would be a bit more involved than they thought.

Cutting down the mistletoe was a big enough job on its own, but once the boys realized they had been working atop a large, sloping hill, they wondered how they were going to haul their cargo back to the house. Even though we were in California and there was no snow, the boys figured the grass could provide the same slick surface and allow them to zip home quickly down the hill, mistletoe ... in tow.

For the tutorial and everything need you to make this quilt visit:
www.msqc.co/blockholiday15

Not one of the boys had much luck in this part of the plan: one hit a tree, another hit a post, and Josh slid under a barbed wire fence right into a rose bush! When they finished getting the mistletoe home they were exhausted, but the mistletoe still had to be washed, bagged, and tied with a pretty ribbon.

The following day they loaded up a wagon and started selling door to door. I dressed them alike in red sweatshirts with large Christmas trees machine appliquéd on the front with lots of

buttons for ornaments. Who could resist a bunch of cute kids with big smiles? They ran out of inventory quite quickly.

When the boys got home they counted up all the money, which seemed like quite a big haul to them. But then they decided to divide the money among everyone who helped. They had to pay the pickers, the ribbon tiers, and the wagon pullers, so nobody ended up making all that much in the end. There was just enough money to go to the dollar store and buy gifts for each other.

You can bet those dollar store gifts were a big deal for the kids after everything they went through to earn them. But I suspect that the better reward was the story my boys have told repeatedly of the year they had the brilliant idea to sell mistletoe.

materials
makes a 73" X 83" quilt

QUILT TOP
- 1 roll of 2½" print strips
- 1 roll of 2½" white strips *or* 1¾ yards cut into 2½" strips

INNER BORDER
- ¾ yard

OUTER BORDER
- 1¼ yards

BINDING
- ¾ yard

BACKING
- 5 yards

SAMPLE QUILT
- **Church Ladies Aprons** by Mary Mulari for Penny Rose

1 sew and cut

Sew a white 2½" strip to a print 2½" strip. **1A** **Make 21.**

Cut the sewn strips into 4½" increments. Each strip will yield (9) 4½" squares. You need 8 squares for the blocks. Set the left over square aside for another project. **1B**

Cut the squares from corner to corner once on the diagonal.

Note: All must be cut in the same direction. **1C**

Each strip set will yield enough triangles to make four blocks. Two will have the reverse coloration of the other two.

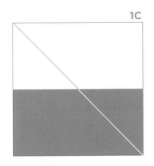

1C

2 make blocks

Select 4 triangles and sew them together as shown. Notice the white pieces form an X.

Make 42. 2A

Select 4 triangles and sew them together as shown. Notice the print pieces make up the X.

Make 42. 2B

Block size: 5" finished

2A

3 arrange in rows

Arrange the blocks into rows. Alternate the blocks that have a white X in the center with a block that has a print X in the center. **Make 14 rows** with each row having 12 blocks.

Sew the rows together once you are happy with the placement of the blocks.

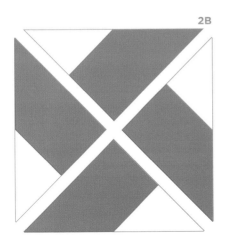

2B

4 inner borders

Cut (7) 2½" strips across the width of the fabric. Sew the strips together end-to-end to make one long strip. Trim the borders from this strip.

Refer to Borders (pg. 100) in the Construction Basics to measure and cut the inner borders. The strips are approximately 70½" for the sides and approximately 64½" for the top and bottom.

5 outer borders

Cut (8) 5" strips across the width of the fabric. Sew the strips together end-to-end to make one long strip. Trim the borders from this strip.

Refer to Borders (pg. 100) in the Construction Basics to measure and cut the inner borders. The strips are approximately 74½" for the sides and approximately 73½" for the top and bottom.

6 quilt and bind

Layer the quilt with backing and batting and quilt. After the quilting is complete, square up the quilt and trim away all excess batting and backing. Add binding to complete the quilt. See Constructions Basics (pg. 101) for binding instructions.

1 Sew a white 2½" strip to a print 2½" strip. Cut the sewn strips into 4½" squares. Step 1.

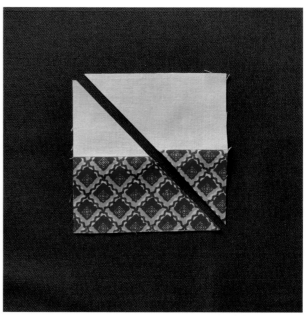

2 Cut the squares from corner to corner once on the diagonal. Each square must be cut the same direction. Step 1.

3 Select 4 triangles that, when sewn together, will make a white X. Lay them out as shown and stitch them together. Step 2.

4 Select 4 triangles that, when sewn together, will make a print X. Lay them out as shown and stitch them together. Step 2.

Dutchman's *puzzle*

quilt designed by JENNY DOAN

People often ask how I met my sweet husband, Ron. Our love story began many, many years ago at a church dance. I was just seventeen years old and Ron was twenty-one.

In those days, my style was that of full-blown hippie. I had long, straight hair parted in the middle and wore a flowing maxi dress and sandals to the dance. Ron, on the other hand, looked very mature and dapper in his white bell bottom pants with a three-inch cuff and his long-sleeved navy blue shirt with gold buttons. He has often told me that when he saw me dancing and laughing with my friends, he fell in love instantly. My first impression of him was slightly less dazzling. Poor Ron was so shy, he could barely finish a sentence! (He was awfully cute, though!)

Shortly after that first meeting, Ron left town for an extended mission trip, and we didn't see each other again for several years. Our second meeting took place at the church as well. I had driven to the Sunday meeting, but my car was acting up and I was a little stressed. As luck would have it, Ron just happened to be at church that same day, and he offered to help with the car. In the days that followed, we spent quite a lot

For the tutorial and everything
you need to make this quilt visit:
www.msqc.co/blockholiday15

of time together talking and enjoying one another's company. We soon became best friends, but when Ron worked up the courage to propose, I wasn't sure how to feel. Oh, I knew he would be a good husband and a wonderful father, but I wanted to feel madly, passionately in love with him - and I didn't. Ron was persistent and assured me that he would love me so completely that I would learn to love him back. So I agreed and put my trust in his love.

Years have passed, and I can see that Ron kept his promise perfectly. He adores me and treats me like a queen, and I can't help but love him with my whole heart. He is such a

completely good man, and he fills my life with fun and happiness.

Looking back I can see that my young self was so caught up in the idea of a white knight on a noble steed that I didn't recognize the man of my dreams when he finally did show up. Love doesn't have to be a fairytale romance that sets your heart ablaze. Real love, true love is what develops when two people care enough to cherish one another. The strongest of trees grow slowly over the years, adding ring upon ring through times both joyful and difficult. My love story may have had a slow beginning, but it's one that has become "Happily Ever After" in every sense of the phrase.

Ron and Jenny circa 1977. When Ron and Jenny met, neither of them knew how much their lives would change or how sweet their love would be.

materials

makes a 81" X 99" quilt

QUILT TOP
- 1 package (40 ct.) print 10" squares
- 1 package (40 ct.) neutral 10" squares

SASHING
- 2 yards

CORNERSTONES
- ¼ yard

OUTER BORDER
- 1¼ yards

BINDING
- ¾ yard

BACKING
- 7½ yards

SAMPLE QUILT
- **New Wave** by Caryl Bryer Fallert Gentry for Benartex

1 making the block

On the reverse side of each of the neutral squares, draw a line from corner to corner twice on the diagonal. **1A**

Place a neutral square atop a print square with right sides facing. Sew ¼" on either side of the drawn lines. **1B**

After you are done sewing, cut the half-square triangle units apart by cutting the squares in half vertically then horizontally. Then cut on the drawn lines. Press the seam allowance, then open each and press again with the seam

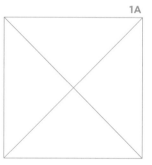

1A

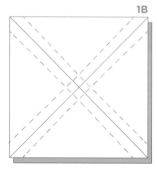

1B

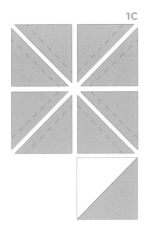

1C

allowance going toward the darker fabric. Trim each unit to 4½". **Make a total of 320 half-square triangles.** 1C

Pair up two half-square triangles that use the same colors. Sew the two together to make a flying geese unit. **Make 4.** Repeat, using a different print. **Make 4.** 1D

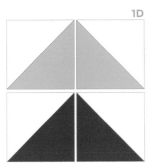

1D

Sew two flying geese units together as shown to make one quadrant of the block. **Make 4.** 1E

Sew the four quadrants together to complete one block. **Make 20 blocks** using various color combinations. 1F

Block size: 16" finished

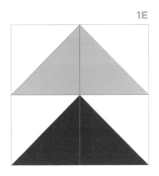

1E

2 cut

From the sashing fabric, cut:
- (49) 2½" x 16½" rectangles

From the cornerstone fabric, cut:
- (30) 2½" squares

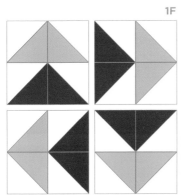

1F

3 sew and arrange

Sew a sashing rectangle to the right side of each block. **Sew 4 blocks** together into a row. Add a sashing rectangle to the left-hand side of the row. **Make 5 rows** in this manner. 3A

Make 6 horizontal sashing strips. Begin with a 2½" cornerstone and alternate with a 2½" x 16½" rectangle. Continue on in this manner until you have sewn 5 cornerstones and 4 rectangles together. 3B

Sew the rows together beginning with a horizontal sashing strip. Alternate with a row of sashed blocks. Continue on in this manner until you have sewn all the rows together. The last row sewn in place should be a horizontal sashing strip. 3C

4 outside border

Cut (9) 4" strips across the width of the fabric. Sew the strips together end-to-end to make one long strip.

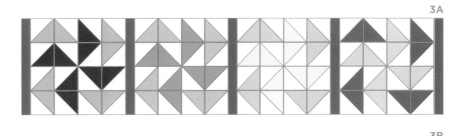

3A

3B

1 Layer a background square with a print square. Draw a line from corner to corner twice on the diagonal. Sew ¼" on either side of the line. Cut the half-square triangle units apart by cutting through the square vertically, horizontally and on the drawn lines. Step 1.

2 Pair up 2 half-square triangles that use the same colors. Sew the two together to make a flying geese unit. Make 2 flying geese units for each of the 4 quadrants of the block. Step 1.

3 Lay out and sew the four quadrants together to complete the block. Step 1.

4 Add sashing strips to either side of each block. Make a long row of sashing, using cornerstones between each sashing rectangle to go between each row of blocks. Step 2.

Refer to Borders (pg. 100) in the Construction Basics to measure and cut the borders. The strips for the sides are approximately 92½" and the strips for the top and bottom are approximately 81½".

5 quilt and bind

Layer the quilt with batting and backing and quilt. Square the quilt as you trim the excess backing and batting away. Add the binding to finish. See Construction Basics (pg. 101) for binding instructions.

*For the tutorial and everything
you need to make this quilt visit:*
www.msqc.co/blockholiday15

square dance

quilt designed by JENNY DOAN

My family loves to dance, which I think is rooted in fond memories of my parents dancing together. When I was a young girl, my parents were a part of a several square dancing groups, and it was probably just as much fun for me as it was for them. I swooned over the outfits: the shoes were shiny gold or silver and the dresses were big and fluffy with full netting petticoats underneath. I loved to watch how they swished and twirled.

I was just a little girl then, and as life went on, Mom and Dad got busy and had to give up their square dancing clubs. But they never gave up dancing; they just moved from the dance hall to the kitchen. And so it has always been for my family too.

Having initially met at a dance, my relationship with Ron started with dancing, and thankfully, in all the years since, we've never stopped. At one point we even took real dance lessons and we loved it. The only hiccup was that I had such a hard time letting Ron lead! (I know, I know, you're shocked, right?) Still, today when one of our favorite songs comes on, Ron gives me that look, holds out his hand, and says, "You wanna dance?" We push back the kitchen island and the rest is history!

I've been thrilled to find that my kids seem to have the same dancing gene I inherited. As they've grown we've held innumerable impromptu kitchen dances. When swing

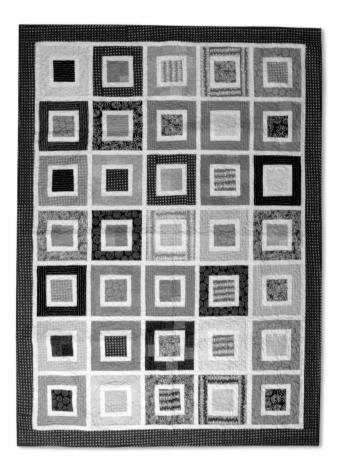

A young Frank and Deannie Fish instilled in Jenny a love of dancing that still endures to this day

dancing came back into style in the 90s, the boys picked it up and wowed me with their moves. I couldn't decide whether to laugh or cry tears of joy at Jake's wedding when he and Alan danced together. It was hilarious and so much fun!

I may have started out loving Mom's square dancing dresses and shiny shoes, but today I can see that what I really love is the freedom, the love, and the togetherness that dancing brings. Our current location and/or ability are irrelevant. Dancing has tied my family together in ways we'll never forget. I hope my kitchen tile is always well-worn from doubling as a dance floor.

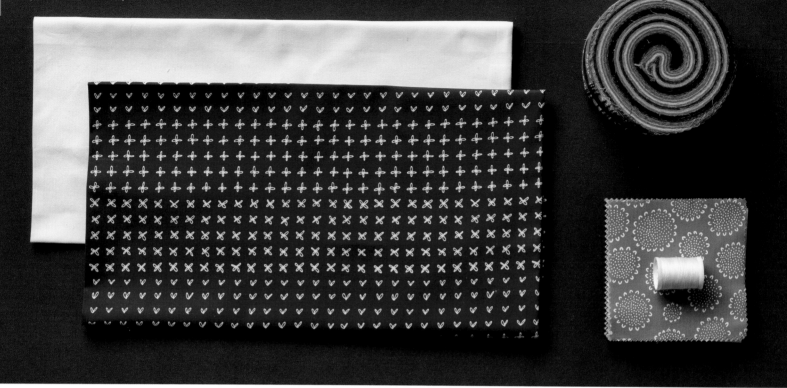

materials
makes a 67½" X 90½" quilt

QUILT TOP
- 1 package 5" print squares
- 1 roll of 2½" strips
- 2¼ yards background – includes fabric for blocks, sashing and inner border

OUTER BORDER
- 1¼ yards

BINDING
- ¾ yard

BACKING
- 5½ yards

SAMPLE QUILT
- **Blueberry Park Cool Colorstory** by Karen Lewis for Robert Kaufman

1 cut

From background fabric, cut:
- (48) 1½" strips across the width of the fabric.

From (31) strips, cut:
- (70) 1½" x 5" A rectangles
- (70) 1½" x 7" B rectangles
- (28) 1½" x 11" rectangles for vertical sashing strips

Set aside the remaining strips for horizontal sashing and inner border.

Select 35 strips from the roll.
From each, cut:
- (2) 2½" x 7" C rectangles
- (2) 2½" x 11" D rectangles

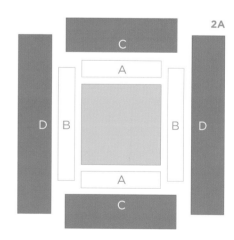

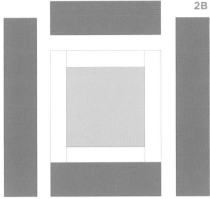

2B

2 block assembly

Lay out the block pieces beginning with a 5" print square in the center. Arrange 2 background A rectangles, 2 background B rectangles and a matching print set of 2 C rectangles and 2 D rectangles as shown. **2A 2B**

3 arrange and sew

Stitch the pieces in place in alphabetical order to complete 1 block. **Make 35.** 3A

Block Size: 10½" finished

4 arrange blocks

Arrange the blocks into 7 rows with each row made up of 5 blocks with a vertical sashing strip placed between each block.

Measure the row horizontally and make 8 horizontal sashing strips that length (approximately 1½" x 57").

Sew the rows together and add a horizontal sashing strip between each row. Then sew a strip to the top and one to the bottom of the center. 4A

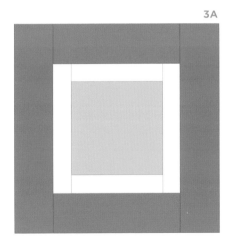

3A

Measure the quilt through the center vertically. Make 2 vertical sashing strips that length (approximately 1½" x 82"). Sew one to either side of the quilt.

5 outer border

Cut (8) 5" strips across the width of the fabric. Sew the strips together end-to-end to make one long strip. Trim the borders from this strip.

Refer to Borders (pg. 100) in the Construction Basics to measure and cut the outer borders. The strips are approximately 82" for the sides and approximately 68" for the top and bottom.

6 quilt and bind

Layer the quilt with batting and backing and quilt. After the quilting is complete, square up the quilt and trim away all excess batting and backing. Add binding to complete the quilt. See Construction Basics (pg. 101) for binding instructions.

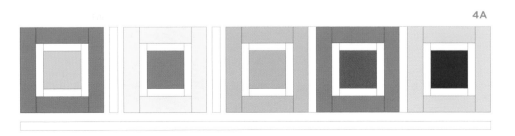

4A

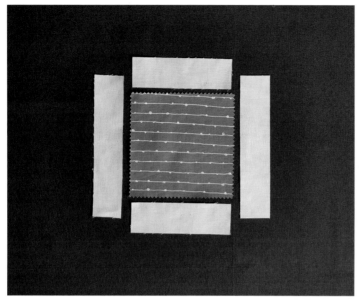

1 Lay out 2 light A rectangles and 2 light B rectangles around a print 5″ square. Step 2.

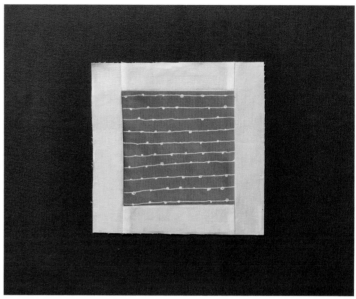

2 Sew the A and B rectangles to the center square. Step 2.

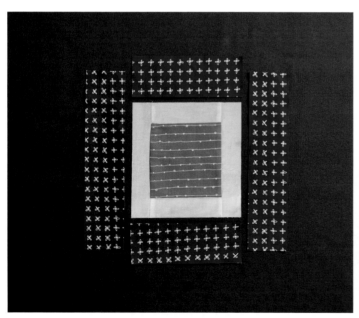

3 Lay out the C and D strips around the center square. Step 2.

4 Sew the C and D pieces in place to complete the block. Step 2.

hard
candy

table topper designed by JENNY DOAN

I get some interesting reactions when folks find out that I have seven kids. "Seven?" they repeat with wide, disbelieving eyes. I love responding with a lighthearted joke. "Of course seven! I hate to cook, so I needed enough kids to cover dinner each night of the week!"

The thing, though, is that's hardly a joke. I have never enjoyed cooking, and I believe in teaching children to work. So naturally, as soon as the kids were old enough to boil macaroni and spread peanut butter and jelly, they were given kitchen duty!

The evening's lucky victim had a comprehensive list of responsibilities. First, the assigned child had to decide what he or she would like to prepare for dinner. Then we looked through the grocery ads together to make a list and go shopping. (Keep in mind there were nine mouths to feed. It is quite the task to plan even the simplest meal on such a large scale!) With the recipe and ingredients ready to go, I worked with the chef of the night as we prepared dinner together. Looking back, I think it

For the tutorial and everything you need to make this quilt visit: www.msqc.co/blockholiday15

was one of the best things I ever did as a parent. It lightened my load considerably, and at the same time the kids learned to cook.

Of course, it didn't take long before a spirit of competition crept in. There were always arguments about whose dinner was the best and whose was a flop. Finally, we decided to hold an official contest, "The Doan Family Bake Off." Each of the kids had to plan and prepare a dessert on his or her own without any help from Mom. And we invited a few families from our church to act as judges to avoid any parental bias.

Each judge was presented with a plate of seven small servings of dessert. They were identified solely by number - no names. The judges carefully tasted and considered each dish as my hopeful contenders looked on. Each child received a prize: "Most attractive dessert," "Stickiest concoction," "Most creative use of corn flakes," etc. Despite the fairness for everyone, there was an actual winner, and that winner received a grand prize. It was such fun that we continued the tradition for many years. We have so many wonderful memories of Doan Family Bake Offs, and, best of all, we now have several amazing cooks in the family. You really should come by sometime for dessert!

The Doan family has always loved to bake together.

"I believe in teaching children to work. So naturally, as soon as the kids were old enough to boil macaroni and spread peanut butter and jelly, they were given kitchen duty!"

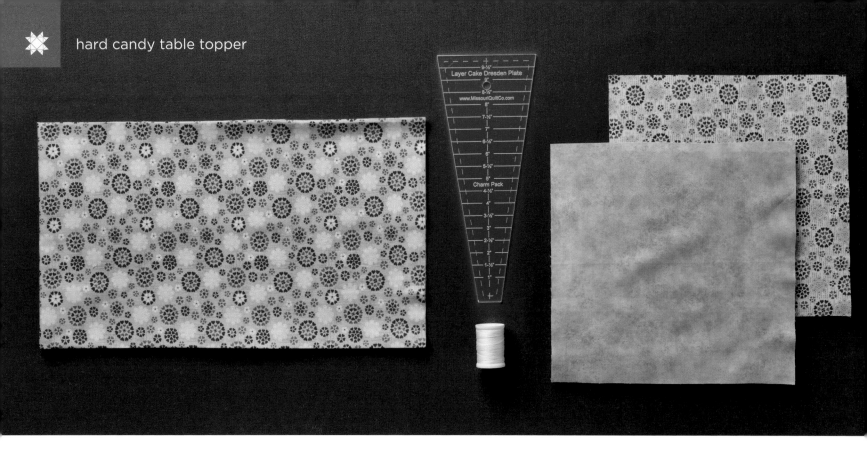

materials

makes an 24" circle table topper

TABLE TOPPER
- (4) 10" squares print
- (4) 10" squares background
- (1) 5" square for circle

BINDING
- ¼ yard *or* (1) 18" square if making continuous bias binding.

BACKING
- ¾ yard

ADDITIONAL SUPPLIES
- MSQC Large Dresden Plate Template
- (1) 5" square fusible interfacing

SAMPLE TABLE TOPPER
- **Hugs and Kisses** by Studio E

1 cut

From the 10" print squares, cut **10 blades** using the template and your rotary cutter. Each square will yield 3 blades provided the direction of the template is flipped with each cut. **1A**

From the background squares, cut **10 blades** in the same manner as above.

From the 5" square, cut 1 circle using the template provided on page 37. From the fusible interfacing, cut (1) 3½" circle using the template provided on page 37.

2 sew

Sew the blades together, alternating a background blade with a print blade. After adding the last blade, close the last seam.

1A

TEMPLATE

2A

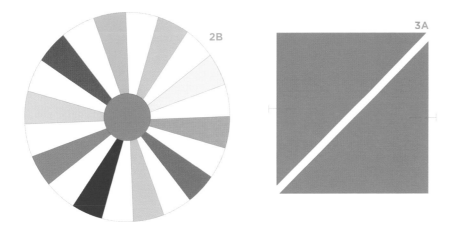

Put the 2 circles together with right sides facing and sew ¼" inside the outer edge. Make a slit in the circle made of fusible interfacing just large enough to turn the circles right side out. Press and appliqué the circle to the center to complete the block. 2A

Layer the block with backing and batting and quilt.

When the quilting is finished, trim the excess batting and backing away and bind. See Construction Basics (pg. 101) for the instructions for applying binding. If you would prefer to use bias binding, follow the instructions below to learn how to make continuous bias binding. 2B

3 continuous bias binding

Cut a square piece of fabric. The size of the square determines how much binding you can get. Multiply the sides of the square by each other, then divide by the width of the binding strip you wish to use. If you cut an 18" square and are making 2½" wide binding, multiply 18 X 18. That equals 324. Divide by 2.5. Your square will yield approximately 129.6" of 2½" wide continuous bias binding.

After you have cut the square, place a pin at the center point on both the right and left sides of the square. Cut the square from corner to corner once on the diagonal. 3A

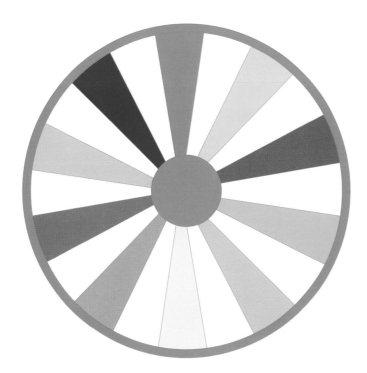

use the outside of this
diagram as 3½" circle template

1 We made our sample using prints and whites. But another option would be to use all prints. In either case, cut 20 blades using the MSQC template. If you chose to use half background blades, alternate them with prints and stitch them together.

2 Cut two 3½" circles, one from print fabric and one from fusible interfacing. Stitch the two together with right sides facing and stitch ¼" inside the outer edge. Cut a small slit in the interfacing and turn the circle right side out. Step 2.

3 Sew the two bias triangles together along the pinned edge. Step 3.

4 Match up one side of the fabric with the first drawn line of the other side. Notice that the tube is "offset." Sew the top and bottom of the tube together and press the seam open. Step 3.

5 Start cutting at the offset (uneven) end of the tube on the drawn line. Cut through only one layer at a time and you will end up with one long strip of continuous bias binding. Step 3.

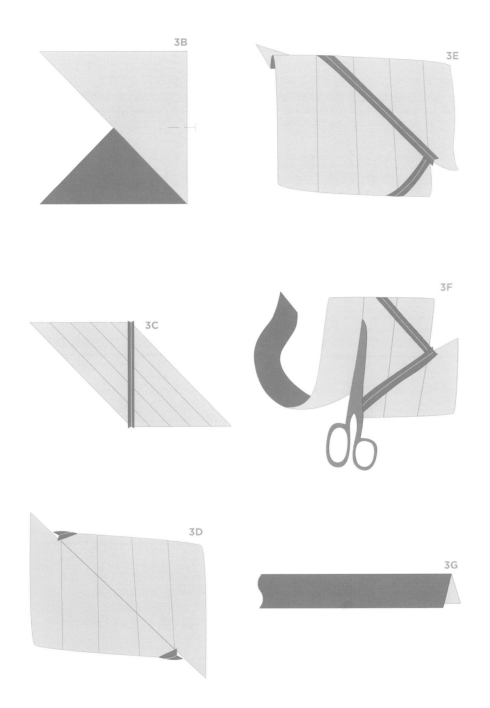

Place the two triangles together with right sides facing. Match up the two pins and sew the two pieces together along the same edge as the pins are placed. 3B

Gently press the seam open. When working with bias edges, it's important not to stretch or pull on the fabric. Use an acrylic quilter's ruler and a fine pencil to mark lines the width you intend to make the binding on the reverse side of the fabric. If you are making 2½" wide binding, you will mark your lines 2½" apart. 3C

Bring the top and bottom pieces of the fabric together to make a tube. Match up one side of the fabric with the first drawn line of the other side. Notice that the tube is "offset". Sew the top and bottom of the tube together and press the seam open. It may feel a little awkward but it works like a charm. 3D 3E

Use a pair of sharp scissors and start cutting at the offset (uneven) end of the tube on the drawn line. Only cut through one layer and continue to cut until you have cut the entire tube apart. You will end up with one long continuous strip of binding. 3F

After you have finished cutting along the lines, begin at one end and fold the strip in half with the wrong sides facing. Press the fold in along the entire strip, again being very careful not to stretch it or pull it out of shape. 3G

For the tutorial and everything you need to make this quilt visit:
www.msqc.co/blockholiday15

boho
baby

quilt designed by NATALIE EARNHEART

Years ago a prominent toy company manufactured a baby doll with a very unusual feature: a hospital nightgown that dissolved in water to reveal the baby's birth certificate, which stated whether the baby was a boy or a girl. Gosh, what if that's how it really worked?

"Doctor, is it a boy or a girl?"

"Well, we'll just have to wait until the birth certificate is ready. We're rinsing it in warm water now."

I know many of the parents who bought those dolls wished they could choose which gender they got so they wouldn't end up with a disappointed little girl at home, set on having a boy or a girl doll. As a mother, I felt for them. I often wished I could pick the gender of the next member of our family, and I rarely got what I wished for. But thank heaven I didn't get to pick! All those surprises made our family into exactly what it needed to be, and I can't imagine us any other way.

My first baby was Natalie, a pink and perfect baby girl. Girls were so much fun that I went ahead and had Sarah just fourteen months later. Of course, after two girls I knew I'd have a boy, so I was surprised to get Hillary! When we finally got a boy we decided he needed a playmate, so Alan

and Jake came along in quick succession. By then I was ready to wrap everything up with one more girl, so naturally we welcomed baby Josh! Along the way we adopted our son Darrell and our family was complete!

In life, we don't always get what we've hoped for, but we often end up with something better than that for which we could have planned. Families, and even quilts, are sometimes best when the result surprises you.

materials

makes a 43" X 48½" quilt

QUILT TOP
• 2 packages of 5" print squares

INNER BORDER
• ¼ yard

OUTER BORDER
• ¾ yard

BINDING
• ½ yard

BACKING
• 3 yards

ADDITIONAL SUPPLIES
• MSQC 5" Tumbler Template

SAMPLE QUILT
• **Urban Zoologie - Nature** by Ann Kelle for Robert Kaufman

1 cut

Using the tumbler template and your rotary cutter, cut:

• 77 tumblers

2 sew

Join the tumblers into vertical rows made up of 11 tumblers, offsetting the seam allowances of each tumbler by ¼" as shown. **2A**

Make 7 rows and stitch them together vertically.

After all the rows have been joined, trim the top and bottom of the quilt so the edges are even. **2B**

2A

2B

3 inner border

Cut (4) 1¾" strips across the width of the inner border fabric. Sew the strips together end-to-end to make one long strip. Trim the borders from this strip.

Refer to Borders (pg. 100) in the Construction Basics to measure and cut the inner borders. The strips are approximately 37½" for the sides and approximately 34½" for the top and bottom.

4 outer border

Cut (5) 5" strips across the width of the fabric. Sew the strips together end-to-end to make one long strip. Trim the borders from this strip.

Refer to Borders (pg. 100) in the Construction Basics to measure and cut the outer borders. The strips are approximately 40" for the sides and approximately 43½" for the top and bottom.

5 quilt and bind

Layer the quilt with batting and backing and quilt. After the quilting is complete, square up the quilt and trim away all excess batting and backing. Add binding to complete the quilt. See Construction Basics (pg. 101) for binding instructions.

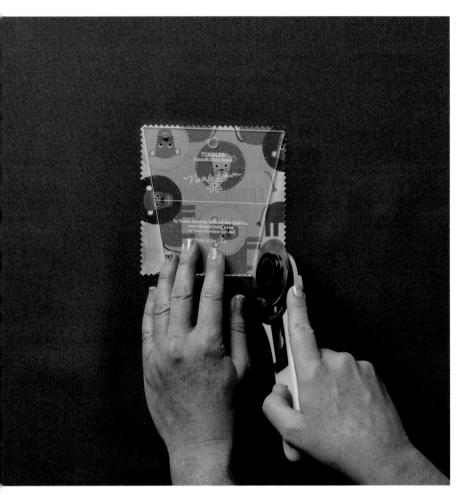

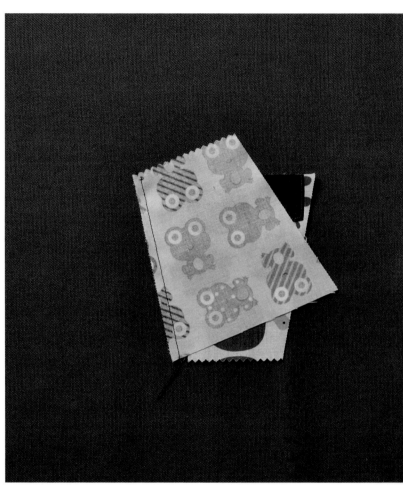

1 Using the 5″ MSQC Tumbler Template, cut 77 tumblers from the 5″ squares. Step 1.

2 Sew the tumblers together. Notice the seam allowance is offset by ¼″. Step 2.

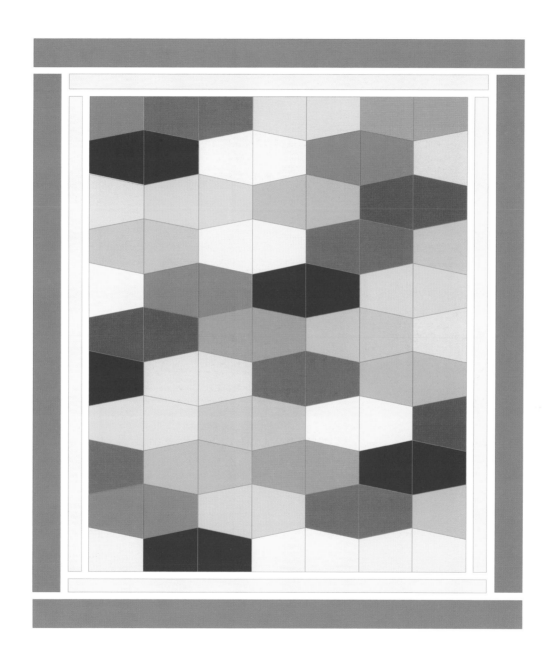

For the tutorial and everything
you need to make this quilt visit:
www.msqc.co/blockholiday15

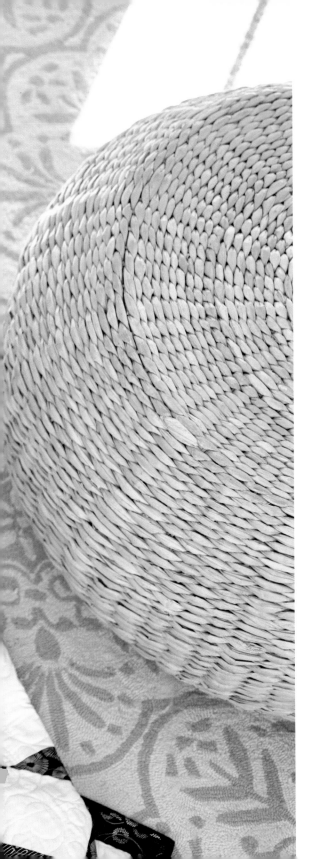

4-patch stars

quilt designed by JENNY DOAN

Christmas morning is a magical time that a child will always cherish, but when money is tight, it takes a bit of ingenuity to create those precious memories. Longtime readers know that when my children were very young, we struggled financially. With Christmas drawing near, Ron and I were determined to find way to fulfill the kids' Christmas wishes despite our lack of means. We couldn't afford a new bike for Alan or a new dollhouse for the girls, but what we lacked in money we made up for in creativity and good, old-fashioned elbow grease. Who needs a brand-new bike when you can gather together all sorts of assorted parts and create a one-of-a-kind, two-wheeled road machine? (We at least hoped Alan would feel that way on Christmas morning.)

With determination in our hearts and paintbrushes in our hands, we went to work. Likening ourselves to Santa and his elves, we set up our secret nighttime workshop. All through the month of December we stayed up late working, sewing, repairing, and painting. By Christmas Eve we were exhausted, but as we set gifts out in front of the Christmas tree, it was a sight to behold! Next to Alan's "bike" sat the four-story doll house Ron and I had made out of plywood scraps. It was furnished with miniature furniture and other fun details, each carefully sanded and painted with love.

An early Christmas morning at the Doans house

The next morning as the children walked down the stairs to see what Santa had brought, there were squeals of delight and surprise. All our hard work paid off as we saw the children's Christmas dreams came true. What a special Christmas that was!

A handmade present is a joy to give. You put so much of yourself into that gift that the payoff is far greater than what you'd experience if you gave a store-bought gift. We quilters know that feeling well. Why else would we dedicate so much time and effort to create something we are just going to give away? It's that moment of surprise and gratitude. It's seeing in their eyes that they truly do love and appreciate your gift. There's just nothing quite like it in all the world.

“ With determination in our hearts and paintbrushes in our hands, we went to work … what we lacked in money we made up for in creativity and good, old-fashioned elbow grease. ”

materials

makes a 74" X 90" quilt

QUILT TOP
- 1 package 10" print squares
- 1 package 10" white squares

INNER BORDER
- ¾ yard

OUTER BORDER
- 1 yard

BINDING
- ¾ yard

BACKING
- 5½ yards

SAMPLE PROJECT
- **Sparkle Studio** by Robert Kaufman

1 half-square triangle units

Select 20 print and 20 white 10" squares. On the back of each of the white squares, draw a line from corner to corner twice on the diagonal. Layer a white square with a print square with right sides facing and sew ¼" on either side of the lines. Cut through the center of the square both vertically and horizontally, then cut along the drawn lines. You need a **total of 160** half-square triangle units. **1A**

Open each half-square triangle unit and press the seam allowance

1A

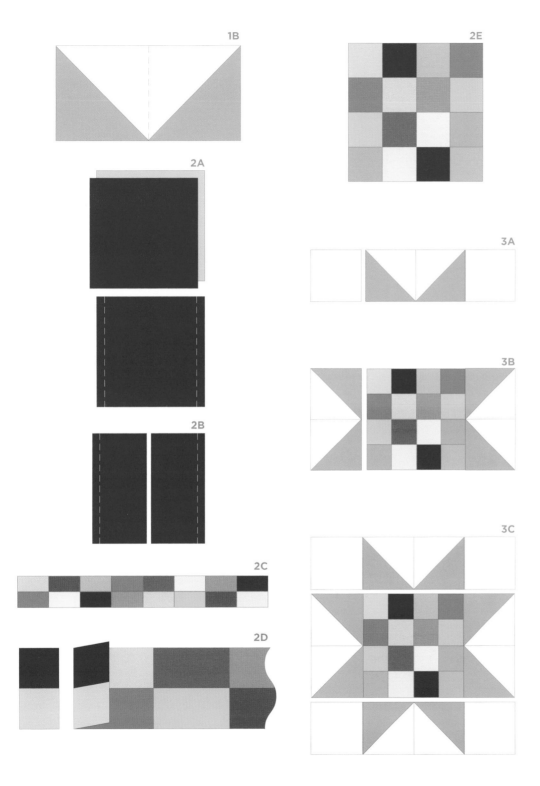

toward the darker fabric. Trim the half-square triangle units to 4½".

Sew the half-square triangles together as shown to make flying geese. **Make 80.** 1B

Cut
- (80) 4½" squares from 20 of the white 10" squares. Set aside for the moment.

2 4-patch units

Cut the remaining print 10" squares in half vertically and horizontally to make 5" squares. Layer two contrasting 5" squares with right sides facing. Sew them together along two sides as shown using ¼" seam allowance. 2A

Measure 2½" from the outer edge of the sewn 5" squares and cut them in half. 2B

Open the units and press. **Make 80**.

Sew the units together end-to-end into a long strip. 2C

Cut (1) 2½" piece from the first segment of the pieced strip. Fold the remaining half of the first segment, with right sides facing, over the next segment in the pieced strip. Cut along the edge of the folded piece as shown. Continue folding and cutting the squares into 4-patch units. **Make 80**. 2D

Sew (4) 4-patch units together to make the center of each star block. **Make 20.** 2E

1 Stitch two 5″ squares together using a ¼″ seam allowance. Measure in 2½″ and slice them in half. Step 2.

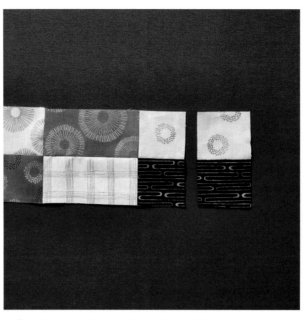

2 Sew the units together end-to-end into one long strip. Cut one 2½″ piece from the first segment, fold the end over and cut along the edge of the folded piece to make 4-patch units. Step 2.

3 Stitch four 4-patches together to make the center of the block. Step 2.

4 Sew a 4½″ square to either side of a flying geese unit to make the top and bottom row of the block. Step 3.

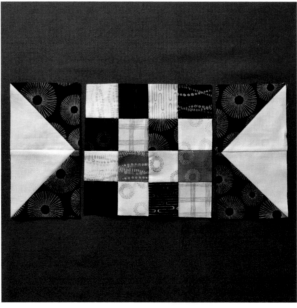

5 Sew a flying geese unit to either side of the center. Step 3.

6 Sew the three rows together to complete the block. Step 3.

3 put it all together

Sew a 4½" square to either side of a flying geese unit. **Make 2 rows** like this for each block. **3A** See pg. 53.

Sew a flying geese unit to either side of a 16-patch. **Make 1 row** like this for each block. **3B** See pg. 53.

Sew the 3 rows together to complete the block. **Make 20**. **3C** See pg. 53.

Block Size: 16" finished

Sew the blocks together into **5 rows of 4**.

4 inner border

Cut (8) 2½" strips across the width of the fabric. Sew the strips together end-to-end to make one long strip. Trim the borders from this strip.

Refer to Borders (pg. 100) in the Construction Basics to measure and cut the inner borders. The strips are approximately 80½" for the sides and approximately 68½" for the top and bottom.

5 outer border

Cut (9) 3½" strips across the width of the fabric. Sew the strips together end-to-end to make one long strip. Trim the borders from this strip.

Refer to Borders (pg. 100) in the Construction Basics to measure and cut the outer borders. The strips are approximately 84½" for the sides and approximately 74½" for the top and bottom.

6 quilt and bind

Layer the quilt with batting and backing and quilt. After the quilting is complete, square up the quilt and trim away all excess batting and backing. Add binding to complete the quilt. See Construction Basics (pg. 101) for binding instructions.

For the tutorial and everything
you need to make this quilt visit:
www.msqc.co/blockholiday15

sunny skies

quilt designed by NATALIE EARNHEART

I usually feel a little sentimental this time of year. My mind wanders back to wonderful holiday memories from my youth. I am proud to say that I was born of good parents. Mom and Dad are now both in their eighties, and I feel so lucky to still have them in my life. They weren't perfect parents, but they were pretty darn close. And they did they best they could, which was more than enough.

As parents we're pretty hard on ourselves. We see our shortcomings and failures, and constantly worry that our efforts don't meet the mark. If you could see yourself through the eyes of your children, however, more often than not you'll

find that the good far outweighs the bad. A magical childhood is one that comprises a lifetime of experiences, stitched together with love. Don't judge yourself so harshly! It's not about perfection. It's about the time and effort and the love you put into doing the best you can.

There is another group of special folks just as self-critical as parents: quilters. Have you ever spent countless hours on a gift only to apologize for its imperfection? I've seen it time and again. It seems that in the midst of praise and thanks, some quilters feel compelled to reject compliments and point out flaws. "Oh, it's nothing special … See how I lost my points here?… And those seams don't quite match up." Why do we do it? We pour our time, energy and love into our quilts! Why do we feel the need to nitpick them so?

If I could, I'd wave a magic wand to cast a spell over your eyes so that you could see your quilts for what they truly are: masterpieces, mistakes and all.

Frank and Deannie Fish. Parents to 6 children, grandparents to 28, and great grandparents to 34 children

materials

makes a 58" x 74" quilt

QUILT TOP
- 1 roll of 2½" print strips
- 1¾ yards gray
- 1¼ yards white

BORDER
- 1¼ yards

BINDING
- ½ yard

BACKING
- 3¾ yards

SAMPLE QUILT
- **Color Union** by RK for Robert Kaufman

1 cut

From the gray, cut:
- (3) 10" strips across the width of the fabric. Subcut the strips into (12) 10" squares.

From the cream fabric, cut:
- (3) 10" strips across the width of the fabric. Subcut the strips into (12) 10" squares.

2 4-patch units

Select (24) 2½" print strips. Make a strip set by sewing 2 assorted print strips together. **Make 12.** **2A** Cut the strip sets into 5" segments. **2B**

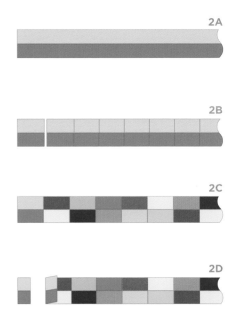

2A

2B

2C

2D

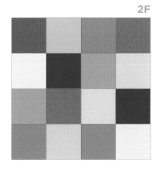

2F

2G

3A

3B

3C

3D

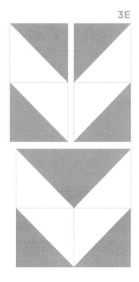

3E

you reach the end of the pieced strip. 2D

You will have (7) 4-patch units and 2 segments. Sew the 2 segments into (1) 4-patch unit. 2E

Repeat for the remaining pieced strips.

Sew (4) 4-patch blocks together to make a 16-patch block. **Make 18.** 2F

Sew (2) 4-patch blocks together to make an 8-patch block. **Make 10.** 2G

3 blocks

Mark a line from corner to corner twice on the reverse side of the white 10″ squares. Place a white 10″ square atop a gray 10″ square with right sides facing. Sew ¼″ on either side of the drawn lines. 3A

Using your rotary cutter and ruler, cut through the center of the squares vertically and horizontally, then on each of the drawn lines. You will have 8 half-square triangle units. 3B

Open the half-square triangles and press the seam allowance toward the darkest fabric. Trim each half-square triangle unit to 4½″.

Repeat for the remaining 10″ squares.

Sew 2 half-square triangle units together as shown to make a diagonal unit. **Make 24.** 3C

Sew 8 assorted segments together to make 1 pieced strip. **Make 12.** 2C

Cut (1) 2½″ piece from the first segment of a pieced strip. Fold the remaining half of the first segment, with right sides facing, over the next segment in the pieced strip.

Cut along the edge of the folded piece as shown. Continue on in this manner until

1 Sew the units together end-to-end into one long strip. Cut one 2½" piece from the first segment, fold the end over and cut along the edge of the folded piece to make 4-patch units. Step 2.

2 Sew four 4-patch blocks together to make each 16-patch block. Step 2.

3 Layer a 10" cream square with a gray square. Draw a line from corner to corner twice on the diagonal. Sew ¼" on either side of the line. Cut the half-square triangle units apart by cutting through the square vertically, horizontally and on the drawn lines. Step 3.

4 Sew 2 half-square triangles together to make one diagonal unit. Step 3.

5 Sew a diagonal unit to a reverse diagonal unit to create a V block. Step 3.

3F

Sew 2 half-square triangle units together, changing the direction of the half-square triangles as shown, to make a reverse diagonal unit. **Make 24.** 3D

Sew a diagonal unit and a reverse diagonal unit together to make a V block. **Make 17.** 3E

Lay out the blocks as shown in diagram 3F. Sew the blocks together into rows. Sew the rows together. 3F

4 outer border

Cut (7) 5½" strips across the width of the fabric. Sew the strips together end-to-end to make one long strip. Trim the borders from this strip.

Refer to Borders (pg. 100) in the Construction Basics to measure and cut the outer borders. The strips are approximately 64½" for the sides and approximately 58½" for the top and bottom.

5 quilt and bind

Layer the quilt with batting and backing and quilt. After the quilting is complete, square up the quilt and trim away all excess batting and backing. Add binding to complete the quilt. See Construction Basics (pg. 101) for binding instructions.

jenny's tents

quilt designed by JENNY DOAN

As a young mom, I constantly looked for little adventures
we could enjoy as a family, so when a friend suggested
rock climbing, I was totally on board. All of the kids were
walking and potty trained - clearly the only prerequisite for
successful rock climbing - and our friends had equipment
and experience. What could possibly go wrong?

Excitedly, we piled into our van and headed south to a well-
known climbing spot near Fort Hunter Liggett Army Base,
in the southern Salinas Valley. Upon arrival, however, my
exuberance began to fade as we walked through the brush
to the base of a cliff, its unwelcoming rocky face staring
down at me. This was no playground jungle gym; this was
the real deal. I looked at my chubby cheeked babes and
wondered how any sane mother would herd them up that
death trap of a climb. I was at the point of turning back, but
our friends encouraged us, promising that all would be well.
So up we went.

*For the tutorial and everything
you need to make this quilt visit
www.msqc.co/blockholiday15*

64

It was slow going up that wall. The little ones struggled terribly, and we were forced to form a human chain to get everyone up. All I could think about was how on earth we were going to get those kids down in one piece! Images flashed before my eyes of headlines reading, "Mother of Seven Kills Children While Rock Climbing!"

As we finally reached the top of the cliff, before we'd even had time to sit down, catch our breath, and take in the view, I started to worry about the descent. However, suddenly my eye caught a glimpse of a windy path in the distance that gently sloped down to the parking lot. How had we not noticed that path before? With newfound energy (Hooray! We're not dead!), we marched down to safety.

When we got back to the car, I spread out a quilt and the family sat down for a picnic. As we ate, we talked about our adventure, agreeing that all in all it had been a good experience. We had learned to trust one another and work together to reach our goal safely. None of us could have done it alone. The drive home was among the most peaceful of my life, with seven sleepy children worn out from a combination of physical exertion and pure terror!

Would we try rock climbing again? Maybe not. Probably not. Okay, never in a million billion years. But we learned important lessons and made terrific memories, so we declared the day a success.

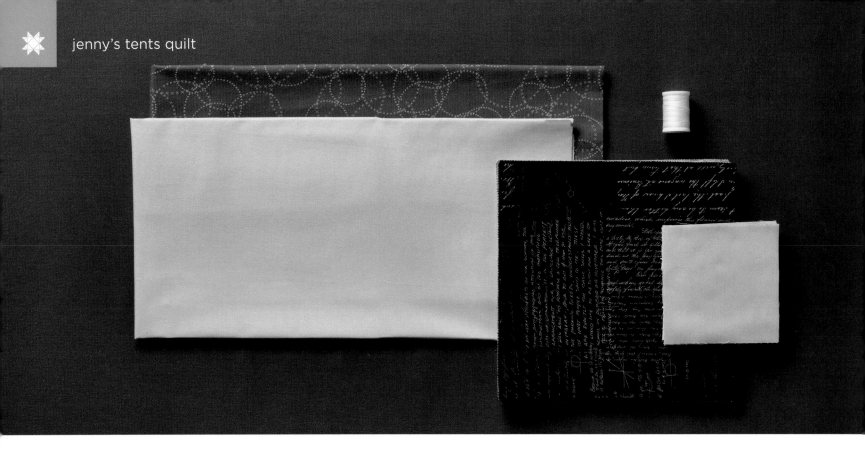

materials

makes a 59" X 67" quilt

QUILT TOP
- 1 package (42 ct.) 10" squares
- 1 package (42 ct.) *or* 1 yard of neutral cut into 5" squares

INNER BORDER
- ½ yard

OUTER BORDER
- 1 yard

BINDING
- ¾ yard

BACKING
- 3¾ yards

SAMPLE QUILT
- **Modern Background** by Zen Chic for Moda Kaufman

1 cut

Cut each of the 5" squares in half twice – once vertically, once horizontally to make a total of **(168)** 2½" squares. **1A**

2 sew blocks

Separate the 10" squares into two stacks, one of light fabrics and the other of darks. On the reverse side of each light square, draw a line from corner to corner twice on the diagonal. **2A**

Place a light square atop a dark square with right sides facing. Sew ¼" on either side of the drawn lines. **2B**

1A

2A

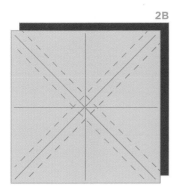

2B

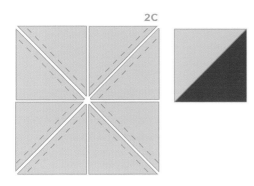

2C

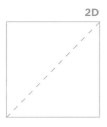

2D

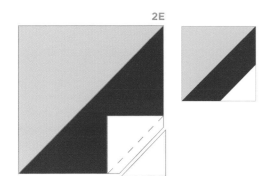

2E

After you are done sewing, cut the half-square triangle units apart by cutting the squares in half vertically, then horizontally. Then cut on the drawn lines. Press the seam allowance, then open each and press again with the seam allowance going toward the darker fabric. Trim each unit to 4½". **2C**

Fold and press each neutral 2½" square in half with right sides facing. The crease will be your sewing line. **2D**

Stitch a neutral 2½" square to the darkest side of a half-square triangle with right sides facing. Sew on the creased line. Trim the excess fabric away ¼" from the seam allowance. Press the seam allowance toward the dark fabric. You will need a total of **168 blocks.** **2E**

Block Size: 4" finished

3 arrange and sew

Sew the blocks together into rows. Each row consists of 12 blocks. **Make 14 rows. 3A**

Press the odd numbered rows toward the right and the even numbered rows toward the left.

Stitch the rows together to complete the center of the quilt.

4 inner borders

Cut (6) 2½" strips across the width of the fabric. Sew the strips together end-to-end to make one long strip. Trim the borders from this strip. Refer to Borders (pg. 100) in the Construction Basics to measure and cut the inner borders. The strips are approximately 56½" for the sides and approximately 52½" for the top and bottom.

5 outer border

Cut (7) 4" strips across the width of the fabric. Sew the strips together end-to-end to make one long strip. Trim the borders from this strip.

Refer to Borders (pg. 100) in the Construction Basics to measure and cut the inner borders. The strips are approximately 60½" for the sides and approximately 59½" for the top and bottom.

6 quilt and bind

Layer the quilt with batting and backing and quilt. After the quilting is complete, square up the quilt and trim away all excess batting and backing. Add binding to complete the quilt. See Construction Basics (pg. 101) for binding instructions.

3A

1 Sew a neutral 2½" square to the darkest side of a half-square triangle. Trim the excess fabric away ¼" from the seam allowance. Step 2.

2 Press the seam allowances toward the darkest fabric. Step 2.

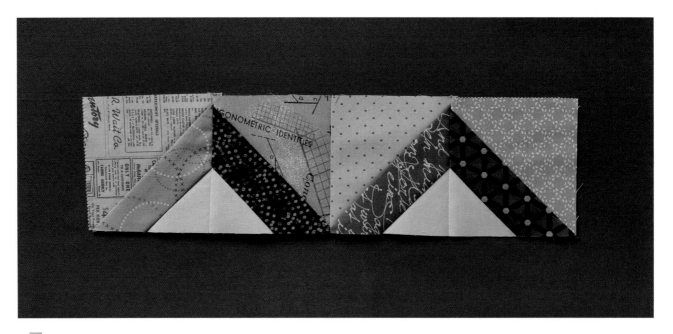

3 Sew the blocks together into rows. Step 3.

For the tutorial and everything you need to make this quilt visit:
www.msqc.co/blockholiday15

hunter's
star

quilt designed by JENNY DOAN

If you've quilted much, you know the feeling you get when you've been working too long on a quilt. I call it QFD: Quilting Frustration Disorder. QFD can cause all kinds of symptoms, including but not limited to going totally nuts! For example, have you ever gotten mad at your sewing machine? Cursing at inanimate objects is definitely a symptom of QFD. And something about sewing the same block a thousand times (give or take nine hundred) gives you such strong QFD goggles that you can't see the block properly anymore. That's when you start making silly mistakes.

This is one of the reasons I try to simplify patterns enough that they come together quickly before you stop having fun or go too crazy with ideas. My problem is that sometimes in the process of simplifying a pattern, I get a touch of QFD and the goggles come on. And the only cure I know for QFD goggles is a fresh pair of eyes.

The Hunter's Star is a pattern that came together in an unexpected way for me. For years I wrote it off because it looked too complicated. (And you know me - I like my quilts quick and easy.) If I can't make it into a simple tutorial for you, I keep looking.

Then I noticed it was starting to pop up online. Quilters were finding tricks to simplify the construction of this beautiful block. So I took another look. I started breaking it down and looking for the best way to show you how to do it. Our pattern writer wrote it up, we made it, and we got ready to film the tutorial.

But before we could get it to YouTube, our videographer, my son Jake, stopped me in my tracks: "Why are you teaching it like this? It's just a four patch and this next block is just a quadrant that rotates…" Suddenly the goggles came off. I could see it! So I remade the quilt as it is here and I think we finally got it just right! All it took was the wisdom of a scruffy young man whose specialty is filming.

I learned a valuable lesson from this quilt. If at first you don't succeed, ask someone who has no idea what they're doing! You'll stave off QFD and you just might get your best idea yet!

"If at first you don't succeed, ask someone who has no idea what they're doing!"

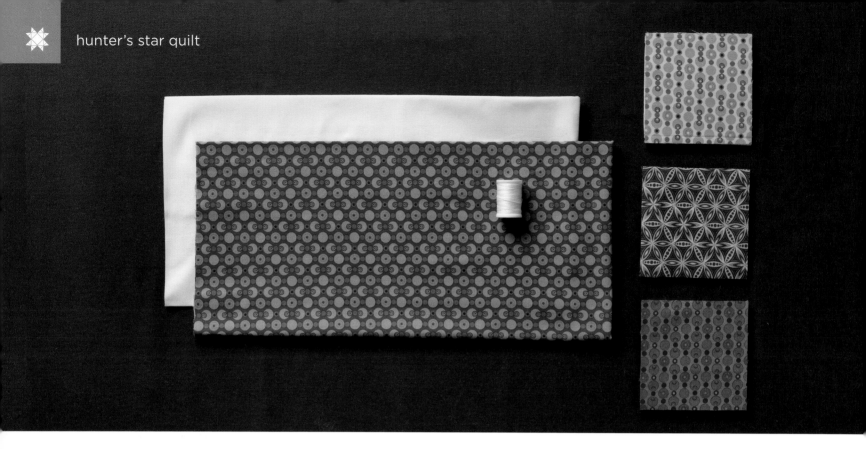

materials

makes a 77 X 86" quilt

QUILT TOP
- (3) packages 5" print squares
- 3¾ yards background – includes blocks and inner border

BORDER
- 1½ yards

BACKING
- 7¼ yards

BINDING
- ¾ yard

SAMPLE QUILT
- **Transformation** by Sarah Vedeler for Benartex

1 cut

From the background fabric, cut:
- (21) 5" strips across the width of the fabric. Subcut into 5" squares for a **total of 168.**

2 make half-square triangles

Pair up a print 5" square with a background 5" square. With right sides facing, sew all around the outside edges using a ¼" seam allowance. Cut through both layers from corner to corner twice on the diagonal. Open each half-square triangle unit and press toward the print fabric. Each pair yields 4 HST. **Make 16** for each star block, **448** for the quilt. **2A**

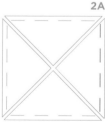

2A

76

3A

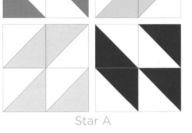

3B

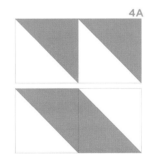

Star A

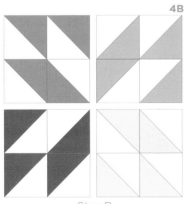

4A

4B

Star B

Square each half-square triangle to 2¾".

3 make star a

Sew 4 half-square triangles together to make one quadrant of Star A. **Make 4.** 3A

Sew the quadrants together to complete Star A. **Make 16**. 3B

4 make star b

Sew 4 half-square triangles together as shown to make one quadrant of the block. Notice the color arrangement of the half-square triangles has changed from Star A. **Make 4.** 4A

5A

Sew the four quadrants together to complete Star B. **Make 12.** 4B

5 make 4-patch blocks

Sew a background 5" square to a print 5" square. **Make 2.** Press the seam allowance to the print fabric. Sew the two together as shown to complete the 4-patch block. **Make 28.** 5A

Block Size: 9" Finished

6 arrange and sew

Sew the blocks together into 8 rows of 7 blocks. Row 1, 3, 5 and 7 all begin with Star A block and alternate with a 4-Patch block. 6A

Rows 2, 4, 6 and 8 all begin with a 4-patch block that has been rotated and alternate with a Star B block. 6B

Press the seam allowances in the odd rows toward the left and the even rows toward the right. Sew the rows together.

6A

6B

1 Layer a print 5″ square with a background 5″ square and sew all the way around the outside edge using a ¼″ seam allowance. Cut the squares from corner to corner twice on the diagonal. Open and press the steams toward the darkest fabric. Step 2.

2 Sew 4 half-square triangles together to make one quadrant of Star A.

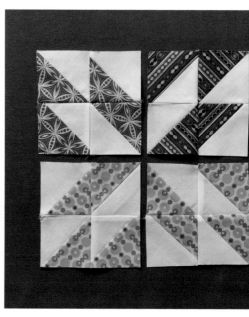

3 Sew the 4 quadrants together to complete Star A.

4 Sew the half-square triangles together as shown to make one quadrant of Star B. Step 4.

5 Sew 4 quadrants together as shown to complete Star B.

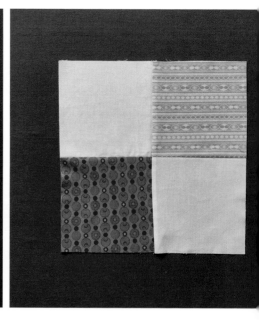

6 Sew four 5″ squares together to make 4-patch units. Step 5.

7 inner border

Cut (8) 2½" strips across the width of the fabric. Sew the strips together end-to-end to make one long strip. Trim the borders from this strip.

Refer to Borders (pg. 100) in the Construction Basics to measure and cut the inner borders. The strips are approximately 72½" for the sides and approximately 67½" for the top and bottom.

8 outer border

Cut (8) 5½" strips across the width of the fabric. Sew the strips together end-to-end to make one long strip. Trim the borders from this strip.

Refer to Borders (pg. 100) in the Construction Basics to measure and cut the inner borders. The strips are approximately 76½" for the sides and approximately 77½" for the top and bottom.

9 quilt and bind

Layer the quilt with batting and backing and quilt. After the quilting is complete, square up the quilt and trim away all excess batting and backing. Add binding to complete the quilt. See Construction Basics (pg. 101) for binding instructions.

flock of
geese

quilt designed by JENNY DOAN

Home is where your football team is, right? We love to cheer for the home team, whoever that may be. Right now, of course, we love the Kansas City Chiefs, but mostly, we just love football. In fact, for me, football is one of the best things about Thanksgiving, and I have one special team to root for no matter where I live.

For years we've had the same Thanksgiving traditions. We get together with Ron's family and have a feast to remember. You've never seen so many Doans in one place! And ever since the kids were little, we've had our own little Turkey Bowl football game in the yard while the kitchen bustles with grown-ups cooking.

For the tutorial and everything you need to make this quilt visit:
www.msqc.co/blockholiday15

To make sure the littlest child can still be part of the fun, we play flag football instead of tackle (which also helps cut down on those pesky trips to the emergency room!). I love watching my kids have a good time: sweaty-faced, out of breath, and smiling ear-to-ear. But the very best part for me, as a mom and now a grandma, is when a bigger kid slows down to let a little one grab a flag, or when one of the big kids picks up a little one and runs him or her in for a touchdown. Nothing brightens Thanksgiving more than a little kid bursting with Turkey Bowl pride. It warms my heart like few other things can.

In previous years, you'd likely see me on the field getting in on the action, but these days, more often than not, I'm the one watching from the porch, wrapped up in a quilt, and cheering on my very own, permanent home team.

" We love to cheer
for the home
team, whoever
that may be. "

materials

makes a 74" X 84½" quilt

QUILT TOP
- 2 packages (42 ct.) print 10" squares
- 2 package (42 ct.) light 10" squares

OUTER BORDER
- 1½ yards

BINDING
- ¾ yard

BACKING
- 5¼ yards

SAMPLE QUILT
- **Storybook Vacation** by Whistler Studios for Windham fabrics

1 block construction

We need half-square triangle units in two sizes to make the block.

To make the large half-square triangles, select 21 light squares and 21 print squares. Pair a light 10" square with a print square with right sides facing. Sew all the way around the outer edge, using a ¼" seam allowance. Cut the squares from corner to corner twice on the diagonal for 4 half-square triangle units. Open each and press the seam allowance toward the darker fabric. **Make 84** and trim each to 5¾". We'll call the large half-square triangles Unit A. **1A**

1A

unit A

1B

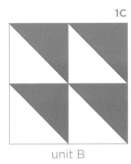

1C

unit B

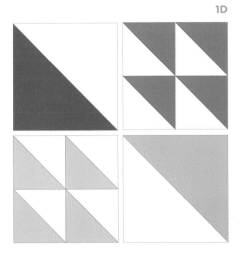

1D

To make the small half-square triangle units, select 21 light squares and 21 print squares. Cut each square in half twice, once vertically and once horizontally, to make (4) 5″ squares.

Pair a light 5″ square with a print 5″ square with right sides facing. Sew all the way around the outer edge using a ¼″ seam allowance. Cut the squares from corner to corner twice on the diagonal for (4) half-square triangle units. Open each and press the seam allowance toward the darker fabric. **Make 336.** 1B

Sew four small half-square triangles together into rows of two as shown. Note the position of the light and dark triangles. Let's call this Unit B. 1C

Make 84.

Sew Unit A and Unit B together. Make two and sew them together as shown to complete one block. **Make 42 blocks.** 1D

Block Size: 10½″ Finished

2 arrange and sew

Sew the blocks together in rows of 6. Make 7 rows, and press the odd numbered rows toward the right and the even numbered rows toward the left.

Sew the rows together to complete the center of the quilt.

3 border

Cut (8) 6″ strips across the width of the fabric. Sew the strips together end-to-end to make one long strip. Trim the borders from this strip.

Refer to Borders (pg. 100) in the Construction Basics to measure and cut the inner borders. The strips are approximately 74″ for the sides and approximately 74½″ for the top and bottom.

4 quilt and bind

Layer the quilt with batting and backing and quilt. After the quilting is complete, square up the quilt and trim away all excess batting and backing. Add binding to complete the quilt. See Construction Basics (pg. 101) for binding instructions.

1   Pair a light 10″ square with a print square with right sides facing. Sew all the way around the outer edge using a ¼″ seam allowance. Cut the squares from corner to corner twice on the diagonal for 4 half-square triangle units. Open each and press the seam allowance toward the darker fabric. Make 84 and trim each to 5¾″. Step 1.

2   To make the small half-square triangles, layer a 5″ light square with a 5″ print square. Sew all the way around the outside edge using a ¼″ seam allowance. Cut the squares from corner to corner twice on the diagonal to make 4 half-square triangles. Step 1.

3   Sew 4 half-square triangles together to make one quadrant of the block. Step 1.

4   Sew the 4 quadrants together to complete the block.

Machine Quilting at MSQC

We have a wonderful Quilting Department here at MSQC, and we'd love to tell you all about it. We currently have about 20 quilters who operate 10 quilting machines full time. On average, we can quilt about 136 quilts in one week. That's pretty impressive, if you ask me!

Here at Missouri Star Quilt Company we offer "all over" or "edge-to-edge" machine quilting. This means that the pattern you choose will be quilted over the entire quilt. This technique lets the quilt pattern shine. If you choose a thread color that blends with your background it will seem to disappear, leaving your quilt looking beautiful and letting the focus be your fabrics and pattern. It looks gorgeous on all quilts, including appliqué and embroidery.

We use state of the art Gammill quilting machines that are equipped with Statler Stitchers. This gives us the ability to offer hundreds of patterns and a relatively quick turnaround time. We strive for good results and we love to see the way machine

quilting can transform a quilt from a flimsy top to a work of art!

We wanted to offer machine quilting services to those who live in areas where they may not have access to a local quilter or to quilters who need the job done in a hurry. Right now you can get your quilt back in about four to six weeks. All this for the low price of 0.02 cents per square inch.

Let me tell you how it works.

When you've finished your quilt top and it's ready for that final step, go to our

website. Look for the machine quilting tab, click and start the process. You'll need to enter the measurements of your quilt. Try to be as accurate as possible. Then choose the thread color and select a quilt pattern from our many quilt designs (you'll be able to see what the patterns look like as you make your choice simply by clicking on the design). Some of our most popular machine quilting patterns are "Loops and Swirls", "Just Roses", and "Champagne Bubbles".

Next is batting, backing, and binding. We

provide the batting free of charge so just choose the type you'd like to have in your quilt. We have a few options available and are hoping to expand with more choices in the future.

Backing can be a bit of a challenge for all of us, so let me share how it works. The Gammill machines that we use have large rolling bars. On these bars are leaders. Those are the strips of heavy-duty fabric that we will pin your quilt to. The quilt gets pinned on in layers so the backing goes on one set of bars, then the batting is laid in, and the quilt top is on a different set of bars. To make them line up properly, we pin all the layers from the top center. This means that your quilt top will lay on the backing about an inch from the top and that both will be lined up on the center point. It's important to have the backing larger than the quilt top so we have room for the edge-to-edge quilt designs as well as the clamps used to keep the backing pulled taut. We especially need the extra length because we don't want to run out of backing before we've finished the quilt top! Ideally your quilt backing will be 8"-10" larger than your quilt top. So if your quilt top measures 62"x78", you would send in a backing that is 72"x 88". You can make your own backing, choose from our wide selection of quilt backs, or have us piece yardage for you.

Binding can be tricky, too. If you prefer to bind your own quilt, we will trim your quilt and send it back ready for binding. But if you want us to bind it, specify which fabric we should use. Be sure there will be enough to complete the job. We offer both hand and machine binding.

Once you've made all your choices, it's time to leave us with any additional comments or instructions.

It's time to package up your quilt and send it to us. We recommend wrapping or bagging your quilt to protect it from moisture and boxing it securely for shipping. We have never had a quilt get permanently lost in the mail, but we still recommend insurance as a protective measure. Please include your order number in the package to ensure we get the right quilt matched up to the right customer.

Once we receive your quilt, it will be checked in and placed on a rack to wait its turn on the quilting machine. We will follow all instructions and get it back home to you as soon as possible. If we run into an issue or have a question, we will email and call you, so be sure your contact info is up to date. We want you to have the best experience possible. We also have a great customer service team that would love to answer any questions you may have. It really is that easy to get your quilt tops finished!

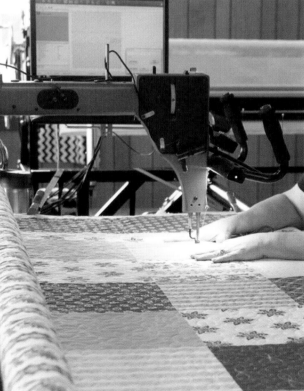

boho
baby

QUILT SIZE
43" X 48½"

DESIGNED BY
Natalie Earnheart

PIECED BY
Carol Henderson

QUILTED BY
Tia Gilliam & Linda Frump

QUILT TOP
2 packages of 5" print squares

INNER BORDER
¼ yard

OUTER BORDER
¾ yard

BINDING
½ yard

BACKING
3 yards

ADDITIONAL SUPPLIES
MSQC 5" Tumbler Template

SAMPLE QUILT
Urban Zoologie - Nature by Ann Kelle for Robert Kaufman

ONLINE TUTORIALS
msqc.co/blockholiday15

QUILTING
Color Me

PATTERN
pg. 40

dutchman's puzzle

QUILT SIZE
81" X 99"

DESIGNED BY
Jenny Doan

PIECED BY
Cindy Morris

QUILTED BY
Mari Zullig

QUILT TOP
1 package (40 ct.) print 10" squares
1 package (40 ct.) neutral 10" squares

SASHING
2 yards

CORNERSTONES
¼ yard

OUTER BORDER
1¼ yards

BINDING
¾ yard

BACKING
7½ yards

SAMPLE QUILT
New Wave by Caryl Bryer Fallert Gentry
for Benartex

ONLINE TUTORIALS
msqc.co/blockholiday15

QUILTING
Loops & Swirls

PATTERN
pg. 16

4-patch star

PROJECT SIZE
74" X 90"

DESIGNED BY
Jenny Doan

PIECED BY
Jenny Doan

QUILTED BY
Jenny Doan

QUILT TOP
1 package 10" print squares
1 package 10" white squares

INNER BORDER
¾ yard

OUTER BORDER
1 yard

BINDING
¾ yard

BACKING
5½ yards

SAMPLE PROJECT
Sparkle Studio by Robert Kaufman

ONLINE TUTORIALS
msqc.co/blockholiday15

QUILTING
Color Me

PATTERN
pg. 48

flock of geese

QUILT SIZE
74" X 84½"

DESIGNED BY
Jenny Doan

PIECED BY
Carol Henderson

QUILTED BY
Linda Frump

QUILT TOP
2 packages (42 ct.) print 10" squares
2 package (42 ct.) light 10" squares

OUTER BORDER
1½ yards

BINDING
¾ yard

BACKING
5¼ yards

SAMPLE QUILT
Storybook Vacation by Whistler
Studios for Windham fabrics

ONLINE TUTORIALS
msqc.co/blockholiday15

QUILTING
Posies

PATTERN
pg. 80

hard
candy

TABLE TOPPER SIZE
24" circle

DESIGNED BY
Sarah Galbraith

PIECED BY
Cindy Morris

QUILTED BY
Cindy Morris

TABLE TOPPER
(4) 10" squares print
(4) 10" squares background
(1) 5" square for circle

BINDING
¼ yard or (1) 18" square if making
    continuous bias binding

BACKING
¾ yard

ADDITIONAL SUPPLIES
MSQC Large Dresden Plate Template
(1) 5" square fusible interfacing

SAMPLE TABLE TOPPER
Hugs and Kisses by Studio E

ONLINE TUTORIALS
msqc.co/blockholiday15

PATTERN
pg. 32

hunter's star

QUILT SIZE
77" X 86"

DESIGNED BY
Jenny Doan

PIECED BY
Natalie Earnheart

QUILTED BY
Sarah Richardson

QUILT TOP
(3) packages 5" print squares
3¾ yards background – includes
    blocks and inner border

BORDER
1½ yards

BACKING
7¼ yards

BINDING
¾ yard

SAMPLE QUILT
Transformation by Sarah Vedeler
for Benartex

ONLINE TUTORIALS
msqc.co/blockholiday15

QUILTING
Meander

QUILT PATTERN
pg. 72

jack & jill

QUILT SIZE
73" X 83"

DESIGNED BY
Jenny Doan

PIECED BY
Kelly McKenzie

QUILTED BY
Daniela Kirk

QUILT TOP
1 roll of 2½" print strips
1 roll of 2½" white strips *or*
    1¾ yards cut into 2½" strips

INNER BORDER
¾ yard

OUTER BORDER
1¼ yards

BINDING
¾ yard

BACKING
5 yards

SAMPLE QUILT
Church Ladies Aprons by Mary
Mulari for Penny Rose

ONLINE TUTORIALS
msqc.co/blockholiday15

QUILTING
Curly Twirly Flowers

QUILT PATTERN
pg. 8

jenny's tents

QUILT SIZE
59" X 67"

DESIGNED BY
Jenny Doan

PIECED BY
Carol Henderson

QUILTED BY
Debbie Allen

QUILT TOP
1 package (42 ct.) 10" squares
1 package (42 ct.) *or* 1 yard of
neutral cut into 5" squares

INNER BORDER
½ yard

OUTER BORDER
1 yard

BINDING
¾ yard

BACKING
3¾ yards

SAMPLE QUILT
Modern Background by Zen Chic
for Moda Kaufman

ONLINE TUTORIALS
msqc.co/blockholiday15

QUILTING
Arc Doodle

PATTERN
pg. 64

square dance

QUILT SIZE
67½" X 90½"

DESIGNED BY
Jenny Doan

PIECED BY
Carol Henderson

QUILTED BY
Tia Gilliam & Linda Frump

QUILT TOP
1 package 5" print squares
1 roll of 2½" strips
2¼ yards background – includes
  fabric for blocks, sashing and
  inner border

OUTER BORDER
1¼ yards

BINDING
¾ yard

BACKING
5½ yards

SAMPLE QUILT
Blueberry Park Cool Colorstory by
Karen Lewis for Robert Kaufman

ONLINE TUTORIALS
msqc.co/blockholiday15

QUILTING
Posies

PATTERN
pg. 24

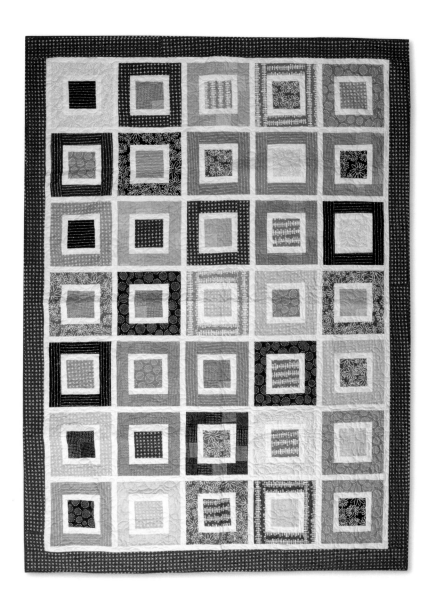

sunny skies

QUILT SIZE
58" X 74"

DESIGNED BY
Natalie Earnheart

PIECED BY
Cindy Morris

QUILTED BY
Linda Frump

QUILT TOP
1 roll of 2½" print strips
1¾ yards gray
1¼ yards white

BORDER
1¼ yards

BINDING
½ yard

BACKING
3¾ yards

SAMPLE QUILT
Color Union by RK for Robert Kaufman

ONLINE TUTORIALS
msqc.co/blockholiday15

QUILTING
Forget me Nots

PATTERN
pg. 56

construction basics

- All seams are ¼" inch unless directions specify differently.

- Cutting instructions are given at the point when cutting is required.

- Precuts are not prewashed; therefore do not prewash other fabrics in the project

- All strips are cut WOF

- Remove all selvages

- All yardages based on 42" WOF

ACRONYMS USED

MSQC	Missouri Star Quilt Co.
RST	right sides together
WST	wrong sides together
HST	half-square triangle
WOF	width of fabric
LOF	length of fabric

pre-cut glossary

5" SQUARE PACK
1 = (42) 5" squares or ¾ yd of fabric
1 = baby
2 = crib
3 = lap
4 = twin

2½" STRIP ROLL
1 = (40) 2½" strip roll cut the width of fabric
    or 2¾ yds of fabric
1 = a twin
2 = queen

10" SQUARE PACK
1 = (42) 10" square pack of fabric: 2¾ yds total
1 = a twin
2 = queen

When we mention a precut, we are basing the pattern on a 40-42 count pack. Not all precuts have the same count, so be sure to check the count on your precut to make sure you have enough pieces to complete your project.

general quilting

- All seams are ¼" inch unless directions specify differently.
- Cutting instructions are given at the point when cutting is required.
- Precuts are not prewashed; therefore do not prewash other fabrics in the project.
- All strips are cut width of fabric.
- Remove all selvages.
- All yardages based on 42" width of fabric (WOF).

press seams

- Use a steam iron on the cotton setting.
- Press the seam just as it was sewn RST. This "sets" the seam.
- With dark fabric on top, lift the dark fabric and press back.
- The seam allowance is pressed toward the dark side. Some patterns may direct otherwise for certain situations.
- Follow pressing arrows in the diagrams when indicated.
- Press toward borders. Pieced borders may demand otherwise.
- Press diagonal seams open on binding to reduce bulk.

borders

- Always measure the quilt top 3 times before cutting borders.
- Start measuring about 4" in from each side and through the center vertically.
- Take the average of those 3 measurements.
- Cut 2 border strips to that size. Piece strips together if needed.
- Attach one to either side of the quilt.
- Position the border fabric on top as you sew. The feed dogs can act like rufflers. Having the border on top will prevent waviness and keep the quilt straight.
- Repeat this process for the top and bottom borders, measuring the width 3 times.
- Include the newly attached side borders in your measurements.
- Press toward the borders.

binding

find a video tutorial at: www.msqc.co/006

- Use 2½" strips for binding.
- Sew strips end-to-end into one long strip with diagonal seams, aka plus sign method (next). Press seams open.
- Fold in half lengthwise wrong sides together and press.
- The entire length should equal the outside dimension of the quilt plus 15" - 20."

plus sign method

- Lay one strip across the other as if to make a plus sign right sides together.
- Sew from top inside to bottom outside corners crossing the intersections of fabric as you sew. Trim excess to ¼" seam allowance.
- Press seam open.

attach binding

- Match raw edges of folded binding to the quilt top edge.
- Leave a 10" tail at the beginning.
- Use a ¼" seam allowance.
- Start in the middle of a long straight side.

find a video tutorial at: www.msqc.co/001

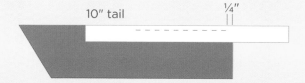

10" tail   ¼"

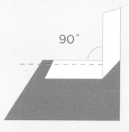

90°   fold

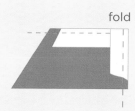

miter corners

- Stop sewing ¼" before the corner.
- Move the quilt out from under the presser foot.
- Clip the threads.
- Flip the binding up at a 90° angle to the edge just sewn.
- Fold the binding down along the next side to be sewn, aligning raw edges.
- The fold will lie along the edge just completed.
- Begin sewing on the fold.

close binding

*MSQC recommends **The Binding Tool** from TQM Products to finish binding perfectly every time.*

- Stop sewing when you have 12" left to reach the start.
- Where the binding tails come together, trim excess leaving only 2½" of overlap.
- It helps to pin or clip the quilt together at the two points where the binding starts and stops. This takes the pressure off of the binding tails while you work.
- Use the plus sign method to sew the two binding ends together, except this time when making the plus sign, match the edges. Using a pencil, mark your sewing line because you won't be able to see where the corners intersect. Sew across.

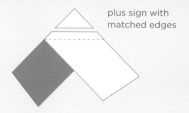

plus sign with matched edges

- Trim off excess; press seam open.
- Fold in half wrong sides together, and align all raw edges to the quilt top.
- Sew this last binding section to the quilt. Press.
- Turn the folded edge of the binding around to the back of the quilt and tack into place with an invisible stitch or machine stitch if you wish.

HIDEAWAY IN QUILT TOWN, USA

PART 5

Calling Home

— *A JENNY DOAN MYSTERY* —

written by Steve Westover

"Well Sean, how'd she do?" Jenny asked impatiently between sips of her strawberry shake. His response was slow, calculated. He said nothing meaningful but appeared nervous nonetheless. Jenny placed one hand on her hip and cocked her head. "Sean, she couldn't have been that bad … could she?"

Sean cleared his throat and looked to the ground. "Well, no. She's actually quite good."

Jenny beamed with pride but despite trying to keep the "I told you so" grin contained her smile broadened around the straw. "That's good to hear," she said plainly.

"On her second day she was our number one call receiver. No complaints. No escalations. I listened to her. She's confident and direct. She's quite charming. She's been our top performer for a few days now."

"That's wonderful," Jenny exclaimed. Then her eyes narrowed as she could tell there was more on Sean's mind. "What is it?"

Sean took a deep breath. "Mom, who is this woman? Where did she come from?"

"What do you mean?" Jenny asked, feigning innocence.

"Well, for starters, she seems over qualified and highly educated for what we have her doing …and … did you know that even though she looks thirty she's really a sixty-two year old grandmother?"

Jenny scoffed. "What are you talking about? That's absurd," she started, but before she could finish her rebuttal Sean continued.

"Background check proves it. When I asked Jin about the discrepancy on her new hire documentation she made up an excuse about having the same name as her mother and that I must have crossed wires somehow."

"Sounds reasonable," Jenny agreed.

"It may sound reasonable but it's not plausible. Social Security Number 'Wires' don't simply get crossed in this way. And it's as if she planned the excuse, like it's something that happens every day. I'm telling you, Mom, something's up and I think you know what I mean."

Jenny waved to the last employee leaving the shop. "See you tomorrow," she called out. Then she and Sean sat as she spilled her guts, recounting Jin's secret. "You can't say anything, Sean. Her life depends on it," Jenny warned.

Sean leaned back in his chair and rested his left ankle on his right knee. "What if she is the fugitive? What if Jin, or whatever her real name is, is putting all of us in danger just by being here? Mom, there's too much we don't know. There's too much risk. She needs to go."

"Go where? She has nothing. She's alone. All she has is us. Sean, I won't abandon her. She needs us. We can help her."

Sean gripped the arms of his chair. "And what if she shouldn't be helped?" The words hovered, polluting the air. "Tomorrow morning I've got to let her go. If you want me to buy her a bus ticket, or take her to Kansas City, I'll do it, but we've got to think about all of our employees, the town, ourselves." Sean shook his head again. "There's simply too much risk."

Jenny's smile had long been replaced by a tight lipped scowl. She considered Sean's position and she couldn't disagree. But she hated it. The thought of refusing someone in need made the bile rise in her throat. She calmed her heavy breathing and then said, "I'll do it."

Sean's eyebrow cocked with skepticism. "Mom, really? I should …"

"I said I'll do it. I'll speak with Jin first thing in the morning and we'll make arrangements for her to leave."

"Make arrangements? Mom, you need to let her go. Immediately."

Jenny stood and walked over to Sean. She bent over and kissed him on the forehead. "Good night. I'll take care of it."

***

Jin arrived early at the call center. She logged into her computer and reviewed her assigned portion of service issues reported by customers online. The fifth customer on her list was from Edison Park on the West Side of Chicago. Jin's service oriented mind slowed as her memories of home flooded in. Remembering her friends, coworkers, her apartment, and even her favorite coffee stand made her nostalgic for her past life that felt so distant. She thought about the turmoil the law firm must be experiencing after Thurman's murder and her disappearance. She longed for home. Jin glanced at her computer and considered the service call she'd need to make to Edison Park.

For days Jin had resisted every urge to search out answers or make contact with anyone from home or work. The threats of the suited men still rang loudly in her mind. Her fear, that they had traced her cell phone on the subway and were likely still searching for her, felt crushing. Unsure of the technical limitations of her pursuers she hadn't dared reveal herself in even the slightest way, not even to the police. She had maintained complete silence. No phone calls. No computer searches. Nothing. But, she was curious about the investigation into Thurman's death. What if the murderers had been captured and she could safely return home? With one simple call her questions could be answered. With MSQC as a cover, she could make that call without revealing her location. She debated internally until a sound interrupted her thoughts.

"You're here early," Jenny said as she walked swiftly across the nearly empty room towards Jin's workstation. Jin startled at the realization she wasn't alone.

"Hi, Jenny. I didn't expect to see you here. I think things are going well. Sean has a good poker face but he seems happy with my work. This job has been a godsend. Thank you, again."

Jenny rolled out a chair from an empty workstation and sat beside Jin. With the motherly eyes in the back of her head she could see Sean standing in the doorway at the back corner of the room and she felt the pressure of his expectations. "Look, Jin, we need to talk." Then Jenny laid out the bad news.

Jin didn't blink or swallow or speak. She couldn't. She had only one thought. Where can I hide next?

As coworkers started filling in the workstations around them, Jenny stood and pushed in her chair. "I'm sorry, Jin. Like I said, you can work through the day to earn a little extra money. Come see me at the main shop when you're done. We'll do dinner and I'll settle up with you. Cash if you want."

Jin nodded. "Yes. Cash, please." She thought for a moment and could feel the eyes of her coworkers on her. "I need to get to work."

"Of course. I'll see you after 6:00," Jenny said and then she walked past Sean and out of the room.

"Mom, why is she putting on her headset? She needs to leave," Sean said as he followed Jenny down the stairs and into the shipping area.

"It's just today, Sean. She needs it. But don't worry. She won't be back tomorrow. You'll never have to see Jin again. No more risk."

***

Jin understood why Jenny did what she did and considered it fortunate to have one last day. Jenny didn't have to allow it and probably shouldn't have. Jin watched the icon on her screen and accepted two calls until she could see that Sean was no longer viewing her screen from his iPad. She toggled over to a Google search and typed in her first query. She found John Thurman's obituary with the time and location of his funeral. It had been yesterday at 2:00. Jin felt empty as she wondered if his killers had attended, pretending to be mourners while searching for her. Then she typed in another search and found a Chicago Tribune article about Thurman's suicide. Suicide? "What?" she exclaimed louder than she intended. She looked around and saw only one co-worker looking in her direction. She glanced back at Sean but his attention was focused out the observation window into the warehouse below.

Jin toggled back to her outgoing call screen and stared at it, determined not to give in to her curiosity. But then, feeling desperate for information, she dialed the phone number of the law firm and quickly added the extension for her closest colleague. She waited

"This is Rachel …" Jin closed her eyes and imagined Rachel on the other end of the call. Rachel spoke again. "Hello … Is anybody …"

Jin swallowed and then blurted out, "Rachel, it's me." She heard a gasp.

"Amber? Is that you?" Rachel asked. It was the first time Jin had heard her real name in over a week. Tears gathered in the corner of her eyes but she fought away the emotion. "Where are you," Rachel asked. "Everyone is worried."

"I'm fine. I can't … I can't say where I am but …" Jin thought about how much she should say and then decided a policy of concealment was still the best plan. "John didn't kill himself," she said, whispering harshly into her mouthpiece. "Two men. Suits. Military hair. I don't know who they are."

Though only seconds, it felt like minutes passed before Rachel spoke again. There was a click, maybe the latch on Rachel's door closing. "No. It was conclusive. The coroner …"

"No, Rachel, listen. I was here. I saw it." Jin's voice grew louder, more agitated. "Two men. They're after me. Has anyone new been hanging around?"

Rachel chuckled nervously. "Amber, there was a death here. Yeah, there have been all kinds of people in and out over the past week; police, crime scene investigators, even the FBI. What else would you expect?"

"FBI … for a suicide? Think, Rachel. That doesn't make sense. Has anyone been in my office or asking about me?" Jin asked but then there was a click. Then another. Not waiting for an answer, Jin hung up and then ripped off her headset and tossed it on the desk beside her monitor. She quickly powered off her computer. Jin's breathing raced as she thought about the "click". The first click could have been the door like she thought, or maybe a faulty connection. But multiple clicks? Jin inhaled a long, soothing breath and then whispered to herself, "Don't be paranoid. No one's tracing the call. No one's trying to find me."

Noticing Sean strolling in her direction Jin quickly stood and strode to the drinking fountain and then the restroom to regain her composure. She stared into the mirror, tightened her ponytail and then chuckled at her skittishness. The call had been risky and yielded her no information but then she reminded herself that even if the killers came looking for her she would be long gone, not by choice, but long gone nonetheless.

Refocusing on her job, Jin sat down at her workstation, plastered on a convincing customer service smile, and plugged on toward 6:00.

***

Two suited men sat in a dark, windowless Mercedes van in the parking lot of a hotel three blocks from the Greyhound Bus Line in Kansas City, Missouri. The engine idled and the driver sat straight with his hands on the wheel, ready for action. The second man hunched in front of a laptop connected to a soundboard at the rear of the vehicle. He removed the thick headphones and then rubbed the stubble above his ears.

"Well?" the driver asked. "Where to?"

His partner typed Missouri Star Quilt Company and the prefix 816 into his laptop. He pressed enter and then smiled. "Hamilton, Missouri. One hour north."

The driver stepped on the gas, rocketing the van into traffic in front of an approaching SUV. "Call the boss. We end this today."